Singing Lessons

Singing Lessons

Poems by

Lin Nelson Benedek

Cover design by Shay Culligan:

Cover photo by Tom Benedek, from the Tom Benedek
Photographic Archive, Special Collections,
W.E.B. Dubois Library, University of Massachusetts, Amherst

ISBN: 978-1-952326-58-5

Kelsay Books
502 South 1040 East, A-119
American Fork, Utah, 84003

This is dedicated to the ones I love

Acknowledgments

I would like to thank the publications in which these poems first appeared:

KYSO Flash: "In the Minute clinic at the CVS"

SoFloPoJo: "They Named our Streets for Saints and Angels"

Curator Magazine: "Benediction"

Dirty Girls Magazine: "Diminuendo," "Forget Everything I Am About to Say"

The Lake: "Architecture: (a) as History;(b) as Aphrodisiac," "Life Lessons from Art History"

Poetry Superhighway: "The Summer my Parents Got Divorced"

Thimble Literary Magazine: "What Could Be More Necessary than Poetry or the Sea"

Third Wednesday: "What's Left"

The quotation featured in my poem "In the Minute Clinic at the CVS" is from a poem by Robert Frost, "A Late Walk," published in 1915 in his book *A Boy's Will* (Henry Holt and Company).

"What Could Be More Necessary than Poetry or the Sea" includes lines from Longfellow's "The Sound of the Sea" and Leigh Hunt's "Abou Ben Adhem."

Gratitude always to my brilliant and generous mentors and professors at Pacific University for initiating me into the brave, beautiful world of poetry—Kwame Dawes, Dorianne Laux, Vievee Francis, Anna Journey, Sandra Alcosser; Joseph Millar, Marvin Bell, David St. John, Ellen Bass, Tyehimba Jess and Eduardo Corral.

And to Heather Lyle, opera singer, jazz singer, vocalogist, for sharing her joyful spirit and abundant gifts, and for nurturing in her students a true love of singing for its own sake.

Deepest love and appreciation to my treasured family, friends, poetry sisters and brothers and teachers.

Tommy and Nicky—forever—my heart and my soul.

Contents

IV

Every word was once a poem.
  —Ralph Waldo Emerson

Every poem was once a song.

I

Cantabile

The tongue is the devil and must be
tamed and trained, Heather tells us—words
of the Italian singing master of a distant century
who warned of all things that *corrupt the voice.*

But she believes
otherwise.

She tells us to plant our feet and keep our knees soft.
First to breathe.
When in doubt belly out.
We whisper *Repetition Repetition Repetition*

I was scared off singing
when I was three.
My grandmother took me to a pastor
and choral director when Dad said I had perfect pitch. I didn't know
Jesus Loves Me,
or any church songs. I sang *Twinkle Twinkle.* I was afraid—of him,
the pipe organ, the cavernous
church. Even God.

Heather runs us through warm-ups
from across centuries
and the world.

Up and down the scales:

Bumble bee-ee
Bumble bee-ee
Bumble Bumble Bumble bee

My mother said she couldn't carry a tune,
but I loved to hear her sing.
She said she was tone deaf, but I loved
her tone, breathless and slightly off-key.

Someday he'll come along. The man I love.
And he'll be big and strong. The man I love.

We yell
jam-Ba! jam-Ba!
as
to a distant friend.

Staccato
Leggato
Tessatura
Coloratura

Words and sounds roll around in our mouths.

Filar al suono. Spin the sounds, Heather says,
spinning her hands

My grandmother said she couldn't
carry a tune. Wanted to be like her
mother, Gee Gee, who sang hymns
around the house while she worked.

Praise God for whom all blessings flow.
Praise Him all creatures here below.
Praise Him above, ye heavenly hosts.
Praise Father, Son and Holy Ghost.

On to more consonants
Hit that jive, Jack

I'm a little witch we say in head voice,
like cartoon villains.

I'm a little elf.

I'm a big troll
in low chest voice

Diaphragmatic breathing
makes the rib cage grow.
Let your jaw go, she says. *Say duh.*

Don't try to think your way out of a self-made prison.
It takes a shock; or a sizzle becomes
a slow burn; or joy builds until you can hold it in
no longer. And the realization that you were never not free.

Grab a catch breath on the fly.

II

Don't try to sound pretty,
Heather says.

*When you love it
more than you fear it,*
Heather says,
you do it anyway.

III

When you catch me
breaking into song.

What's Left

Nine muses, no prisoners
One silver feather, not the bird it flew in on
A bronze pinecone, no gold medal
One pale green ceramic grasshopper, no mercy
A bottle from France, no tomorrow
A solitary earth-sphere of lapis lazuli, no elf to drink it
One little yellow teapot, no promises
An ancient Chinese fisherman, no time
One teal *oroborus,* no moon
No gilt, no filigree, ten photographs
of ones you love, no exceptions,
no deathbed confessions

Portrait of the Artist as a Young Woman

Is this is the girl in all her messy glory?

Yes, this is the girl in her messy glory.

No, she does not play that guitar.

Yes, the photographer is in love with the girl.

She does comb her hair, sometimes,

yes, and the girl did just have her way with the photographer.

Yes, she made that dress herself, on her grandmother's Singer.

Yardage, yes, courtesy of Calico Corners.

Is that *Blood on the Tracks?* Yes.

And Modigliani's *Woman with Cigarette* tacked to the wall? Yes.

It is 1975. Yes.

Next in queue: Coltrane in Paris.

Yes, most definitely a *Deutschegramofon* album cover on the receiver,

Tristan and Isolde spinning on the turntable.

And yes those are her Winston's.

Does the girl have everything she needs? Yes.

The girl has everything she needs.

Go Tell Aunt Rhody

My brother Tony sneaks a trick cigarette into Mom's Alpine's and I half want to warn her. She's riding in front with Dad, four kids in the back of the Lincoln Continental, color of champagne. We leave Victoria for Seattle on schedule. 5:30 a.m. Little Stevie makes up verses for *Birdie, Birdie in the sky.* I stare at the back of Dad's head and catch him giving Mom the stink-eye. I've watched him pull her in for a kiss and I've watched her pull away. Susie and I begin to sing. Dad calls us the pixillated sisters. Mom says we're the Greek chorus. We sing the camp and glee club songs Susie taught me. We start with a favorite. *Alas, my love, you do me wrong, to treat me so discourteously.* It's Dad who wants to take us on these driving trips, but he has a temper. Even so, I'm never happier than when we're all together. Dad wants to show us the world; wants to make good time; has it all mapped out. The breakfast place for the best French toast in the world. The German deli for the best pastrami. The best steakhouse or fish place for dinner. We're happiest at mealtimes. Dad makes jokes. Mom smiles again. Back in the car Susie and I start up again: *The ash grove how graceful, how plainly 'tis speaking...* As we head towards Puget Sound the family sings a round. *Man's life's a bubble full of woe. Man breaks the bubble down he goes. Downie Downie Downie Downie Down he goes.* The other hotels at capacity for the World's Fair, we get rooms at the Calhoun, where, in the lobby, old men smoke cigars and the man at the newsstand sells used magazines. We walk to a fish place in the neighborhood. Stop on the way back at a curiosity shop and watch a flea circus under a microscope and see *The Lord's Prayer* carved on the head of a pin. I throw up all night in the bathroom between the bedrooms, kids in one, parents in the other. Bad clams. Through the door I hear Mom and Dad arguing. I can't make out the words but I catch the tone. The next morning, back on the road, I'm not feeling so hot. The singing helps, though it's a sad dirge. Even Dad joins in.

Go tell Aunt Rhody. Go tell Aunt Rhody. Go tell Aunt Rhody the old gray goose is dead. The one she's been saving. The one she's been saving. The one she's been saving to make a feather bed. Mom takes a cigarette from the pack, lights up. We wait. Is it a dud? No scream. No pop. We don't know this road trip will be our last.

Instructions for Surrender

I

Notice the small things. The cat jumping on the keyboard, typing
po\]/[=-/ after your name.

The crow on the patio wall, talking to the cat.

Blue-violet of Hydrangea, deep pink of Impatiens, sweet surprise
of patience when, again, and again, you had to wait.

The undoing, when you give in to a simple stretch you do day after
day.

And the sky, usually blue, you could say today,
everything and nothing combined.

And you feel hope, after a hard few months,

loving whom you love, breathing the air you breathe,
breathing, period.

II

I sit in the patio in a faded blue chair from home.
This garden will not be contained.
I brought as much of it with me as I could.
One rose. One Meyer lemon. Some
favorite flowers will not grow. Matilija Poppies,
Pride of Madeira, Angel's Trumpet. But the herbs
and annuals are small enough to move to the sunniest
spots. Four hundred trees grow on this block. Redwoods
and Eucalyptus; Magnolias and Sycamores.
The cactus has grown two feet in two years.

23

We brought the blue and white urn, the ochre one,
the jade planter, small beige pots with angels
in bas-relief, cement camel, cat sculpture my mother-in-law
carved from stone, verdigris lizard on the brick border.
We put up majesty bells, seashell wind chimes,
filigree mandala found in a corner of the garage
on moving day. Mobile of African animals made
of clay. Colors of sea and sky, sand and coral
and seashells. Blue Agave, Aloe Vera, succulents
in a planter. Jose and Angel helped me plant
Star Jasmine, Westringia, Sweet pea bush,
Geranium bush, Japanese Windmill flowers,
Bougainvillea, Lantana, Begonia. These flowers
love the ocean air, a mile from the water, wetter
and cooler than the dry hills of the canyon.
Paper White blooms break loose
from their plain brown wrappers. We've planted
rosemary, thyme, lavender and sage in painted pots
from Mexico. I rub the leaves between my fingers
and hold my fingers to my nose. Pheromones of flowers.
Birds sing me home.

III

Greedy little suckers, those small orange butterflies slurping juices
from the purple flowers of the Coast Rosemary. Fools for beauty.

I sweep fallen pink-tinged leaves, eucalyptus, and
bones of pine cones left by squirrels. Small red-breasted birds, two
of them,

fly into the patio and sing a while on the edge of the roof, cat still
watching
from inside. Dog's chew-bones in a low empty pot.

The earth is my garden.
The world is my home.

Rockabye treetops on a nestle of redwoods; expanse of sky.
Our son wonders why we'd trade our house in the woods
for a townhouse near the sea.

He is our world. He doesn't know
when you get older you long for sea. You long for sky.

Long Drink of Water

Around 1936, squinting into the sun like a movie star, one leg up on the running board of the 1930 Chrysler roadster, paid for painting houses first summer after college.

Around 1939, pumping gas and checking oil levels at the Texaco. Your first job. Your brothers call you Carrot-Top, Beanpole, Long Drink of Water.

Around 1941, you and mom, married, in the front seat of the new Chevrolet business coupe you drove until war's end. Stripped, no radio, bought on credit for a lot of money in those days. Rebuilt the engine three times yourself. Worst part was keeping it in tires, rubber at a shortage worldwide.

Around 1943, next to the Chevy, a young dad, lifting a baby above your head; asking her how it felt to be so high.

Around 1947, squatting, two babies now, one straddling each knee, in front of a classic: A '46 Ford woody station wagon with a real wood body.

Around 1956, you, singing *Allá en el Rancho Grande.* Our big daddy. At our dinner table you're no one's little brother. Sometimes you pound your fist on the table and make the dishes jump.

Around 1957, you and Hy Lawrence in the yellow and black De Soto, on your way to Shreveport or Tulsa or Houston, hulking oil tanks in the background, calling on truck manufacturers and oil companies.

Around 1961, you and mom in front, four kids
in the back of the Lincoln Continental.
No one's going to tell you what to drive.

Around 1966, after the divorce, standing with Lisa in a parking lot in front of the white Mercedes, about to buy a round of drinks for everyone at the bar.

Around 1978, a Manhattan in one hand, the other resting on the roof of the stretched-out white-on-white Chrysler New Yorker.

Around 1984, about to take off for the morning AA meeting at the Sixth Step House on the old coast road in Leucadia, standing in front of the white Peugeot: an outstanding performer on treacherous roads, ice, snow, off-highway; a great traveling car, reasonably priced, economical to operate.

Around 1992, you in the driver's seat, nothing to prove, and Sam, the black and white spaniel, in the passenger seat of the Subaru SVX with ABS brakes and computer-controlled traction, powerful engine, four-wheel drive. You love a high-end car, but also economy, happy your second wife shares your love of a grocery store bargain.

Around 1995, you, of the racing green Subaru.

Telling me you were born with a wheel in your hand.
Telling me you'll probably stay with the wagon indefinitely.
Telling me you've covered pretty near about a million miles of highway.

Diminuendo

I don't want to know I've shrunk.
You're a sweet man. I like it
that you wear a yarmulke with your
doctor coat.
It makes me feel a bit safer,
like flying with nuns.
My friend said now she's a certain
age she's become invisible. My
singing teacher said No Way
and I said Me, too. You
used to be shy but we're friends
now. The Ted Talk
says women need to take up
more space
in the world. Facebook said
some people, when they
hear your story, contract; some,
when they hear your story, expand.
Now you tell me
how hard it is for you to stop
eating chocolate. Soon, my soul.
My body will be outgrown.

The Summer my Parents Got Divorced

Every morning Dad picks me up at Mom's and drives me to the
plant. We don't talk.

The machine shop smells of oil spills.
Metal shavings stick in my sandals.

Ida May and Mae Belle type invoices for
White Engine Company and Caterpillar and Mack on company
letterhead:
Power Plus Corporation. I don't want to be a secretary.
I fit in with the guys.

Out back, I assemble manuals. *How to Prevent Dipstick Disasters,*
to the whoosh of compressors and hydraulics.

Machinists Juan, Ricardo, Manuel pour
molten aluminum—crackling, liquid silver—into molds. I have a
crush
on Ricky, the cute one.

I tell my mother the plot of *Camelot.* I saw it
with my boyfriend at the drive-in.

When I get to the part where Guinevere tells Arthur *Live! Live!*
we both weep. We hate goodbyes.
Lately there have been too many.

I'm sleeping with my boyfriend. She must know it.

My grandmother teaches me to sew.
I make a backless wrap dress
to wear with combat boots and a short battle jacket.
I put it on for the first time to go to the Free Press Bookstore
in Old Town.

I'm working to pay for the former VP's company car. It will soon
be mine:
A '65 baby blue Mustang convertible. Mom went on two dates with
him
after the divorce, but it's too close to home, and she's nowhere near
ready for this.

The foreman's son goes to Dartmouth. He doesn't think much of
me—the boss's
daughter. *Which literary figure do you identify with the most?* he
asks.

Anna Karenina, I say. You can tell already that romanticism
will be the death of me.

II

In the Minute Clinic at the CVS

We walked down State Street in the snow and rode the escalators to the row of plastic chairs, where I sat with college kids in squall jackets and fleece. Jeremy, the nurse practitioner, called my name and asked where I was from and I said California. He told me he was working on his doctorate, just recently returned from Ghana, where he and a team were training medical staff to go into the field to treat patients in their towns and villages. I said My poetry professor is from Ghana—Kwame Dawes—and sang praises for my teacher. Jeremy told me that Kwame means born on Saturday and said he himself was born on Saturday so that would be his name, too, and here it was, a Saturday. He said he'd been working in Kumasi at the university, named after another Saturday son, Kwame Nkrumah. So you write poetry, he said, and I showed him the link to the cover art of wild horses painted by my mom's hero, Millard Sheets, and he said when he was living in Vermont an old street poet taught him about cadence. He yawned and told me he'd had his young kids, three and five, over the weekend, both down with the flu and puking all night. It wasn't his weekend but he and his ex were still best of friends and he wanted to help her out because she was going through some tough stuff. He asked what had brought me to the clinic and I said something was troubling my eyes. He took my vitals and I said Sometimes I have white coat hypertension in a strange setting. Jeremy put the cuff on my arm and I pictured myself floating on my back in the ocean back home and he began to recite a poem as he listened to the device, saying *When I go up through the mowing field...And when I come up from the garden ground...A tree beside the wall stands bare...I end not far from my going forth...By picking the faded blue of the last remaining aster flower to carry again to you*. I don't know how he managed to deliver a poem with such feeling as he listened to the sounds my heart was making. When he was done I said Oh, that was lovely and he said It's Robert Frost and I asked how my pressure was and he said it was perfect, couldn't have been better, and I told him that was a first and he said It's the poetry cure.

33

Life Lessons from Art History

Chiaroscuro:
Light and shadow will follow you all the days of your lives. Expect it.

Putti:
And I quote: "Little pudgy, rose-cheeked babies, sometimes with wings, shown doing grown-up things like making bread, riding chariots, making wine."

Vanishing Point:
Sometimes it's hard to tell. Are you coming or going?

Perspective:
When you're not seeing straight and someone tells you to look at it from another angle.

Illuminated Manuscript:
Like a comic book or graphic novel, only grander. You'll know it when you see it.

Cloisonné:
Channels set in stone. Life itself is way more complicated.

Sfumato:
Where I might as well be you and you me; where hair becomes sun becomes water becomes clouds becomes rain becomes rivers becomes oceans and we appear and disappear like angels.

Variations on a Text by Donald Justice Called
Variations on a Text by Vallejo

I will die in Miami in the sun…

It will be L.A. It will be raining. It will be
(sorry, Chaucer; you, too, Eliot), February,
the real cruelest month, or perhaps it will be May and not raining,
and it may not be the City of Angels
(a.k.a., *El Pueblo de Nuestra Señora la Reina de los Angeles*) and it
will be of natural causes—
what exactly are unnatural causes?—
and I will have outlived
too many, or not, and
some will be crying and
some will laugh, in spite of themselves,
at inopportune
times and one nephew will say
She taught me to swim and one
niece will say She taught me
to belch
and some will say
Sorry for your loss
and I will miss it all.

I do not want to leave my son.

Lin Benedek is dead.
The rain does or does not come down
on the cars and on the oil-stained, or the newly paved, avenues;
on the bare or hatted heads of the people; on people running
into Jiffy Marts for cigarettes and Sprite, or somewhere else
for something else.

When the last of the mourners are gone
Lin Benedek will leave the living (and/or dead)
to the blessed living (and/or dead.) Some will be
dabbing their eyes and some will be saying She's
better off dead. Some will say She's an angel now.
And some will not.

Pomegranate Boy

I consulted my heart
and all six of my senses.
I picked the guy
with the shy eyes
and the beautiful hands
and he picked me.

What Could Be More Necessary than Poetry or the Sea?

My husband recites long-out-of-favor Longfellow and I know why
I'm here.
Longfellow brought him words and words brought him to me.
Sandpipers scuttle shoreline, tracks in wet sand.

The sea awoke at midnight from its sleep…

And round the pebbly beaches far and wide…

I never thought it was coming for me, this violent, beautiful sea.

"By which magic does the earth breathe?" the professor asks.

"Define the forces of nature, including the fifth we call
quintessence."

Last night we sat out with a crescent moon and a smattering of
stars.
I almost fell asleep to the rhythmic crashing and low hollow sounds,
salt spray in my nostrils
and on the arms of the wooden chair and on the cushions. I'm not
going to pretend. Most of my adventures take place in my
imagination; more ventures inner than outer. I probably shouldn't be
telling you this: Home is my muse.

In the morning dolphins play in the surf close in.
I'm drawn here by the light, bright with no seeing.

Mr. Boynton gave us each a poem to memorize.
"Abou Ben Adhem" was mine.

I pray thee, then, write me as one who loves his fellow man.

After his heart attack, Mr. Boynton reclined on a chaise at the front of the room and taught us about the world.

"Name five coastal towns. Name the seven seas, the seven winds."

Once the forces of nature were one.

We all die sometime.

My first epiphany, at ten: My family, asleep. I'm sitting on a balcony on a cliff in Corona del Mar, looking out to sea at dawn, under the spell of sea-surrender, feeling greater and smaller than I ever have.

We know nothing and we know everything.

All of it and none of it are me. All of it and none of it are mine.

Too Honest to Steal, Too Ugly to Strip

A street guy holds the sign. It lies. He's handsome, unwashed
in a worn-out motorcycle jacket. I loved a boy with a motorcycle
when I was young, rode on the back along winding roads holding
tight
around his narrow waist, smelling the clean brown hair which fell
down
around his shoulders. I heard him call my name from the backstairs.
I came down in my nightgown like a bride, tried not to make
the backstairs creak—his mother so fine and fierce, his father
so stern. We talked in bed and smoked Camels. It wasn't
the disapproval that drove us apart. Somewhere in time we're
sharing a meatball sandwich at a diner by the river, eating
with a runcible spoon. Oh, his kiss. His body. His nature fierce
and complicated, like an elegant math problem. The morning I left
he was sitting at the kitchen table with a cup of coffee. I stood behind
him
and rested my cheek on the top of his head. We didn't speak
but I'm quite sure we cried. The weather contradicts itself today.
The ocean's flat, the sun dim behind gray haze.
At the corner of Artesia and Aviation, heading back from
Redondo, I listen to Marvin Gaye sing *Got to Give it Up* and watch
the inflatable windsock man, red and yellow, dance like crazy
next to the oil change sign at the Shell station. This is the gloomiest
time of year, when everyone leaves—my mother, my father,
my grandmother; and Dutchie, our barge dog, age ten. My friend
said the other day *If we're lucky, we'll have another twenty
or thirty years.*

Piano Recital

Papa Haydn's dead and gone but his memory lingers on.
When his heart was full of bliss he would sing a song like this.

I'm five, in a powder-pink organza dress
my grandmother made for me. It's beautiful,
but not on me, with its defined waist
and flounced skirt. (Little Linnie's
not so little anymore.) My hair's
in Shirley Temple curls. Someone decided
I needed a perm for my straight blonde hair.

To prepare I practiced again and again at Mrs. Cade's
upstairs studio, ready to stop after the first three tries,
but I'm a good girl and do what I'm told. She gives me
gold stars to stick in my piano book.
It's not a brilliant debut.
I play the right notes.
But it's not enough.
You can tell when your mother isn't thrilled.
You can pretend, but inside you know.

Next Mrs. Cade is going to teach me
Hey Ho, nobody home. Meat nor drink
nor money have I none. Unless Mommy
lets me quit piano.

I can't wait to get home and out of my dress.
Home, where I can sneak something sweet.
Home to my kitty, who loves me the way I am.

They Named our Streets for Saints and Angels

I. Begin at the Beginning

My name is Spanish. Lin for Linda for Rosalinda for patron saint of gardens, for living in a little hut in her garden. For pretty. For beautiful. For not always pretty. For never been pretty. For Beau like boy, for Belle like girl. For Rosalinda. Beautiful Rose. For the love of roses. Rose roses. *Roses are rose. Violets are violet.* Rose roses and violet violets.

II. L. A. Inventions:

Hula hoop, Egg McMuffin, Barbie, WD-40, California Rolls, Cobb Salad, the French Dip sandwich, the Shirley Temple, Orange Julius, Nicotine patch

(Note relationship to leisure time, food consumption, cigarettes.)

Good people of Los Angeles, you call yourself City of Angels, but do you know what it takes to become a saint?

III. Making Rain

A confession. We didn't actually make it rain. But it sounded like rain. We rubbed thumb and index finger together, an assembly room of us, children and parents, sitting on the rug at All School Meeting at my son's school. It's miraculous what you can achieve *When two or more are gathered....*

IV. Birds and Other Miracles

Our cat, Mimi, is a bit like St. Francis. God's truth.
Birds flock to her. Her first two years she grew up in a house, our
neighbor's, full of dogs, one free-flying bird and chickens in the
yard.

I imitate the cat imitating birds chattering on our patio.

V. Life and Other Maladies

Mother Teresa was a saint! She, who suffered religious doubt every
day of her life. I, who will never be a saint, imitate myself living the
life I didn't know I'd live.

My brother built an altar for the Sisters of Mercy in Tijuana. He's
not a carpenter. He'd never built an altar. But he did God's work.
And the sisters rejoiced to behold his handiwork. He asked Mother
Teresa to bless medals for his wife and two sisters—Susie (My
sister of mercy) and me. I keep my medal safe. My lapsed Catholic
friend tells me it's a second-degree relic,
second only to the things that touched Jesus, like bone shards or the
Shroud. God and I speak daily, dead serious, and on a first name
basis. My God, and My Jesus, love us equally. Not a soul left
behind.

I prefer my saints merciful and kind. But I'm not going for
sainthood. This medal resting above my heart is the closest I will
come.

VI. Good Works

To become an angel is easy. A lifetime of good works and you're in,
or, if you prefer, you can
redeem yourself after a fall. It's not that hard.

Saint Nicholas, patron saint of prostitutes, was no stranger to the so-
called "whore with the heart of gold."

A stranger asks you the way. You play: *Take Me to the River.*

A stranger asks when you'll get there. *In the Midnight Hour,* you
reply.

A traveler doesn't know which way to turn. You sing: *By the Rivers
of Babylon.*

Tell me. Patron saint of messengers and postal workers?
Bravo! San Gabriel!

VII. Logistics

Angelenos, here, when you give someone directions, it sounds like
a prayer.

*Follow San Pasqual to San Rafael to San Joaquin to San Anselmo
to El Camino Real.*

They just might get there.

*San Pedro, Santa Catalina, San Diego, San Juan Capistrano, San
Francisco, San Luis Obispo, Santa Clarita.*

Get off however and whenever you like.

Saint Anthony, patron saint of lost things, help me to find my way.

I know of few roads named for our first dwellers, although they
must exist:

Chumash, Hahamogna, Tongva.
We kept the Christian names, why? Because Spain. Because
Mexico.
Because the ones with the arms, the purse, the sword.

El Camino Real, La Ballona, Rincon, La Brea.

We, the people, are responsible for our nicknames.

Angeltown, Hell A. Lost Angeles. La La Land.

Grit in our glitter in this town with a past.

VIII. Something for Everyone

ATM machines, a Ralph's on every corner, drive-in churches, Beach
Cities Car Wash—little heaven at the corner of Lincoln and Lucile
where pleasant sounds drown out traffic noise from the boulevard
and all the elements are represented: Earth, Wind, Fire and Rain.

Be an angel. Try for sainthood. *Better the devil you know.*

Forget about orange blossoms. Ambition.
Jim Morrison's lost angels bedeviling the night air. These are
givens.

Never mind the days so bright, the nights so dark.

We've got saints. We've got angels. Hell A is a Goddamn prayer.

III

Benediction

Bless the top of my head
My jukebox brain
My third eye, my eyelids,
Haughty bridge of my nose
My tongue, that old tutor
Lip, sole betrayer
Clavicle, you flirt
Breastbone, my wishbone
Matador heart
Naval, my mother, my origins, my hurt
Gut, roiling, calm, my rogue second brain
My spine, edifice, tower, my snake
Vagina, my love, my sentinel and protector
My sphincter, good sphincter
My tailbone, my vestige, my horse, cow and dog
Workhorse and urchin, my sweet candy ass
Kneecaps, my headlights, my capstones and soldiers
Ankles, Clydesdales, my tournament horses
Arches of triumph, my sweet golden arches
Honkytonk piggies, hilarious brethren
Soles of my feet, tethers and touchstones
God oh my God oh my God
Bless my bones

Bungalow Heaven

Up one flight of stairs you'd catch a sliver of ocean through the tall window at the front corner of the room, three blocks from the beach. In the other direction you could see out to our second story patio to bungalow roofs and the neighbors' overgrown yards and trees. Tom's old stereo was our altar. We were newly and happily in love. But life was hard in other ways. I was working out endless grief and guilt over my mother's death and the after-effects of her divorce. Some years come with a soundtrack. This year was like that. Tracks from *The Harder They Come,* The Band and Taj Mahal; the Rolling Stones and Joni Mitchell; The Meters and Joe Sample, Steely Dan and Stevie Wonder; Bonnie Raitt, Toots and the Maytals, Gil Scott-Heron, Marvin Gaye. Love and music. Joy and pain. I was student-teaching forty-five minutes from home. Tom was writing a script, Orange County Red, and driving for Red Top Cab. We lived on Kraft macaroni and cheese, but spent our last change on little dinner parties, when Tom made stuffed tufoli or moussaka and we carved out a pineapple bowl to use for the fruit. We smoked, drank, danced, fought. It was a record year for sex. We'd taken in two cats. Gracie, black with white markings, and Montana, white with black markings, sister offspring of a feral mother. This was before we knew better than to let them have litters of their own. Our neighbor Gloria witnessed their mating with the same tomcat within minutes downstairs by the laundry room. When it was their time, they gave birth within an hour of each other to five and six kittens respectively. When the kittens were old enough to leave their mothers we found homes for ten of the babies and kept one, Gracie's son Nelson. At the end of the school year Tom spoke the words. "Will you marry me, my peach?" He made a mix tape of the music we'd listened to over the last year to play at the reception. *Sweet and Dandy* was our anthem. This was all I'd ever wanted. To belong. To be home. To be a part of something. To love and be loved and to love the world.

Worry as a Guitar

I strum my worry until the fingers bleed.

This worry does not gently weep. This worry
sighs and goes silent or sobs wracking sobs

which set the body trembling. Once
in a while worry sits in its case.

But I come back, pick it up by the neck
as if to strangle it, dust it off, play the same
chorus, again and again.

Keep it up, my teacher says. All that
fretting builds callouses.

Soon you won't feel a thing.

Faded Signals

Here on earth we call it "poor communication."

Remember when you read me loud?

They say the sounds go on forever, as in
eternity, and immortality.

Word problem:

How many light years does it take for a radio signal
to get to Alpha Centauri?

How long will it take for you to get to me?

Field Notes for a Summer Poem

Let there be
Frogs and ants
Hot pavement
Aloe Vera
Warm breeze

Let there be
Purple flowers
Weathered bench
Reflection of leaves on the underside
Of an umbrella

Let there be
Alcoves for birds
Birds of Paradise
Bird whistle
Bird
Fennel Thistle Morning Glory

Let there be
Native flowers
Wooden planter
Sun on dry wood chips
Green leaf the size of a hand

Let there be
Orange butterflies
Olive trees
Upside-down sunflowers
Right-side up bees

Pretty Gazelles

Rider with a French horn, leaping stag, jaguar, wild boar,
peacocks, forest bear, pretty gazelles.

My mother's treasure box is decorated
with creatures in suspended animation.

It was a gift box for Christmas candy; a container for anxiety
and unpaid bills; thing more than thing.

My husband kept it for loose pennies. Our son used it
for his tyrannosaurus tooth; pencil from the Victoria and Albert

museum—decorated with ladybugs, butterflies, horsetail ferns,
dragonflies; piece of clear plastic in the shape of a pyramid;

Alamo sticker from Texas; puzzle piece—an alligator; a pair
of dice. Things he won't be needing. I'm going to take it back.

What's Mine

"Don't touch anything," Mommy says. I'm three, wandering the aisles of the five and dime, out of view of my mother. I see a carved wooden dog the size of a Matchbox toy, a St. Bernard like Heidi, the dog we gave away, all of us at the edge of the curb crying as the other family drove away like thieves with our family pet. I slip the little dog into my pocket with a rush of nerve and hurry away to another aisle. I see a baby. I can't help myself. I pinch his fat little leg. I don't do it to hurt him. It's not my fault he looks so cute in his sailor suit. His cries drive home my secret badness. Here it is: I love my mother desperately. Dog = love = Mom = x = my little stolen loves. Could I have loved her better? Could I have loved her more?

Christmastime

Picture this: An Old English Sheepdog
in a Santa hat, tied to a fire hydrant outside
Ye Olde Britannia Pub, three blocks
from the ocean in downtown Santa Monica.
A man asks my husband for spare change.
My husband doesn't hear him.
He's deaf in one ear. We stop at a stoplight
with our hoods up. Another man comes up
behind us, *hhhrrumphing* with the cold.
Bet you thought I was Santa Claus, he says.
Ho. Ho. Ho.

IV

Forget Everything I Am about to Say

Be a shy child. Find solace in furry creatures
and rocking chairs.

Fear abandonment. Feel
unlovable. Above all, carry shame.

Smoke too many cigarettes. Find your worth
in the opinion of others.

Die inside
when your mother dies.
Believe me: It's your fault.

Drink. A lot. You'll be bolder on alcohol.

Decide not to love
or need anyone like that again.

Resist philosophy and its easy answers.
Do not make peace with impermanence.

Drive
too fast on mountain roads, coast downhill
with the engine off and rely heavily
on the brakes.

Laugh when others say all you ever wanted
was to love.

Ignore random signs from the universe.

Do your best to override any rosy opinion of yourself.

Try not to watch the geese glide effortlessly
across the surface of the pond.

God Save Our Queen

Queen bees…make a 'piping' noise…like the quacking or tooting noise of a toy trumpet…a G# or an A in pitch….Drones make a popping noise when they mate and then die.

—The Beekeeper's Bible

Hive
politics are a brutal
business. The queen bee is much
fussed over by twelve attendants
who guard, clean and feed her. Her
daughters, the thousands
of foragers,
work themselves to death.
It's true that drones, one hundred to a hive,
battle to learn who will mate with the virgin
queen from another hive.
She herself fights her sisters
to the death for the privilege.
In her mating flight the new queen buzzes
above landmarks—church steeples
or boulders—to find a swarm of drones
to compete for the honor of falling
on the sword for the good of the hive
and meet her pipe with their pop.
A brutal business.
Yes.

More on the Subject of Bees

Where the bee sucks, there suck I.
—Wm. Shakespeare

I cannot speak for all bees,
nor for all poets, hard workers
all. Flowers cannot live without bees.
Not all agree the world
can't survive without poets. The bee
takes what it can and gives it back:
Nectar from clover, from orange
blossoms, buckwheat and tupelo,
apple blossoms, sourwood, sunflowers,
eucalyptus, sage and avocado, basswood,
alfalfa and goldenrod. In return, sweetness,
propagation, sustenance. Likewise the poet.
Sleep and dreams sustain her. Oceans, rivers,
hills and mountains whisper in her ear.

Missing

Neutron star   gobbled by a black hole

Old location of the shifting North Pole   edging away from

the Canadian Arctic
                  towards Russia

Ken's Lariat, where Mom took us for dinner

           when Dad was away

The Yellow Jacket   (we called it Buzzy Buzz Burger)
Henry's Rite Spot Drive-In   (fried chicken in a
basket

                      (biscuits with

butter and honey)

Monty's Steak House   where Uncle Mac and Great-Uncle
Bob

          opened and closed   the bar

Gee Gee's   wedding ring

Ann's   diamond pendant

Lulu   (cat)
Bridey   (dog)

Mimi's house   (the buyers promised it wasn't a tear-
down)

Our house   in the hills

                      American democracy

The belief we are   a righteous nation

My   youth

Dad   gone twenty years

Mom   fifty

Wicked Games

*The harmonica is the best-selling musical instrument of all time. You're
welcome.*

—Bob Dylan

He's a dubious cat, our teacher, around sixty, with Johnny Cash hair
and sideburns. Over the next two hours he's going to teach us
Harmonica for Health and Blues Harp for Beginners.

My husband and I walk in minutes late and the teacher's not happy.
The old lady next to us is hard of hearing.
She says *What'd he say?* Her old man says *Shuddup.*
Overgrown teenagers, like us.

I ask about our teacher's favorites:

"Christo Redemptor," Charlie Musselwhite
"Wicked Games," Gemma Hayes
"Roller Coaster," Little Walter

Have fun with your harp he says.

We want to learn to play like:

James Cotton
Stevie Wonder
Taj Mahal
Tom Petty
The Rolling Stones
The Doors

We're Baby Boomers. We never grew up.

Love your harp he says.

He shows us licks, trills, flutters, draw and blow, air from the throat, pucker vs. tongue block and the almighty tongue slap.

Paint the harp with your tongue in little strokes he says. *Be one with the instrument.*

She wants French kisses.
Pucker won't do he says.

Whoo like an anxious, excited owl.
Did-der daddy is your jam.

Hit those dirty notes.

Hold it with your left
even if you're a rightie.

Fun facts on the back of the Hohner box:

At the Illinois debate Abe Lincoln went toe-to-toe
with Stephen A. Douglass, who had a bandstand
orchestra to back him up. Unfazed, Abe said

My trusty harmonica will do.

At the end of class our teacher hard-sells the practice CD containing all his tricks, so we can hone our Hohner skills in the privacy of home.

The old lady and her man are smiling now.

My old man and I are smiling, too.

Turns out you can teach an old dog new tricks.

Canterbury Records

I am in need of music.
—Elizabeth Bishop

Stevie and I ride there on our bikes.
We choose LP's from bins marked
Rock and Roll, Rhythm and Blues and *Soul.*
Love song lullabies from Motown
and Muscle Shoals; anthems from Stax.
We play them in the sound-proof booths.
Fools for the rhythm section, the strong bass line,
the throbbing beat that goes straight for the heart.
Here is the missing ingredient. Everything
we want our lives to be. Each record a world:
*Natch'l Blues, Surrealistic Pillow, The Doors,
Electric Ladyland, Reach Out, I Never Loved
a Man the Way I Love You.* Soundtrack.
Drug of choice. I want to say salvation.

Architecture: (a) as History; (b) as Aphrodisiac

I

I interview the old man, my father-in-law, about his first eighty
years

and on a napkin, he draws a map of his childhood home,
built around a courtyard in Orashaza, Hungary,

where his father owned the town textile store, called,
in translation, *Young Married Woman of Szeged.*

He says the black décor makes the restaurant *un peu funèbre.* A bit
funereal.

II

Generations come. Generations go.

His father, his father's father, my father, my father's father, all
the fathers.

And all the mothers of all the mothers stayed home.

We sit under the clock in the Beaux Arts station home of the Musée
d'Orsay and visit his old building on Rue des Grands Augustins.

Paris. Home to High Gothic, Flamboyant, Belle Epoque,
Art Nouveau; majesty and ornament.

III

At our hotel French doors lead to a balcony framed in ornate
ironwork.

The sun is rising to extinguish the night. The river is rising.

Citizens are rising all around the city.

The sun is rising. The bread is rising. The steam is rising.

Rising to fill the empty space that waits in my body.

We look toward the window
and see something shimmer
behind the veil.

In a white bedroom in Paris,
hesitation slips through the tiny waist
of an hourglass.

Forsaking allegiance to our separate selves,
we slip into history. We slip into the dream.

Praise Song for Womankind

Praise for my mother. My mother, Madeline, I praise you.
Praise for my sister. My sister, Susie, I praise you.
Praise for my grandmothers and great-grandmothers.
Praise for the soul-daughters, heart sisters and mother figures.
Pray for the enemies, the mean girls, that they be called friend.
Praise the leaders, teachers, girl dogs and girl cats: Gracie, Bridie,
Lulu, Kiki, Star. Praise the sacred. The feminine. Praise the goddess
in her many forms; holy women east, south, north and west. Praise
angels. Praise pathmakers, truthtellers, now more than ever, healers,
brave ones, nurturers and muses. Praise the ones who stood up and
the ones who sat down; the ones who speak up and the ones who
remain silent. Praise our firm hand and our tender touch; our bodies
like thunder and our lightning minds. Praise for our blessed souls.

This Cat Nicky B. is the Mother-Funkin' Truth!

—Fan on Twitter

This cat Nicky B. (our son) has a theory. Seems Stevie Wonder was piped in before birth, when I was still carrying him (our son) in my body, when I wasn't listening to *You Are My Sunshine* on the furry wind-up duck or the songs on the lullabye tape: *All the Pretty Little Horses; Wynken, Blynken* and *Nod; I Gave my Love a Cherry; Rockabye Baby.* Grandpa points to a picture in the music book and the baby says *Balalaika!* Grandpa makes up games to play with the baby. Grandpa cries *Hippsy-Hoppsy! Bingalow-Bungalow!* We read to the baby: *Whiskers and Rhymes. Old Possum's Book of Practical Cats.* He pitches a tent in the pages of these books, the way I did with *A Child's Garden of Verses.* The baby grows up. He goes off to college with his guitar and his bass and his jazz band heart. He learns about waveforms and reverb. Stevie Wonder's the surprise guest in his Stevie Wonder class. Stevie plays some songs. *Love's in Need of Love Today. You are the Sunshine of my Life. As.* Back when, hands on my burgeoning belly, communing with our son-to-be, we asked the baby questions: Are you going to love the mountains and the snow? my husband asked. The answer came back: I like grass and kitties. Still loves grass. Still loves kitties. Will be loving Stevie Wonder always.

In Praise of Men

Bless the boys who made me weak
and the men who made me strong.
Bless the boys who taught me love,
the ones who taught me to forgive.
Bless the man who held my hand.
Bless my brothers. Bless my father.
Bless my husband. Bless my son.

About the Author

Lin Nelson Benedek earned her M.F.A. in Writing at Pacific University in Forest Grove, Oregon. She has had poems published in a number of journals and in six anthologies. Her first full-length poetry collection, *I Was Going to Be a Cowgirl,* was published by Kelsay Books in 2017. Her second poetry collection, *When a Peacock Speaks to You in a Dream,* was published in 2018, also by Kelsay Books. A third-generation Californian, Lin lives with her husband, Tom, in Altadena, under the spell of wildflowers, orange blossoms and the San Gabriel Mountains. Their son, Nicky, lives in nearby Highland Park. A longtime psychotherapist, Lin is passionate about human connection and believes in the power of poetry to heal, connect and transform us. She is working on a memoir called *Love-Starved Girl.*

www.ingramcontent.com/pod-product-compliance
Lightning Source LLC
Chambersburg PA
CBHW071357090426
42738CB00012B/3140